NORTH AMERICA

NORTH
AMERICAN

TROPIC OF CANCER

EQUATOR

SOUTH AMERICA

ATACAMA

TROPIC OF CAPRICORN

PATAGONIAN

DESERTS

SEYMOUR SIMON

MORROW JUNIOR BOOKS
New York

PHOTO AND ART CREDITS

Chuck Place: front jacket, pages 14–15,
16, 17, 19, 20, 21, 23, 24, 27, 28, 32;
John Cancalosi: Back jacket, page 31;
National Park Service: page 9 by Woodbridge Williams,
page 13 by Richard Frear, pages 18 and 30;
Lehman Caves National Monument: page 11;
Arlene Goldberg: endpaper maps, artwork on pages 7 and 8.

Printed in Singapore at Tien Wah Press.

1 2 3 4 5 6 7 8 9 10

Library of Congress Cataloging-in-Publication Data
Simon, Seymour.
Deserts/Seymour Simon.
p.   cm.
Summary: Describes the nature and characteristics of deserts,
where they are located, and how they are formed.
ISBN 0-688-07415-4.—ISBN 0-688-07416-2 (lib. bdg.)
1. Deserts—Juvenile literature. [1. Deserts.] I. Title.
GB612.S56   1990
551.4′15—dc20   89-39738   CIP   AC

To Michael Alan Simon

To most of us, deserts mean sand dunes stretching as far as the eye can see. We usually think of deserts as windy, waterless places under the broiling sun, with few signs of life. Some, such as this part of the Mojave Desert in Death Valley, California, are like that. Many others are quite different.

There are deserts where rain is never seen and others where rain may fall a dozen times a year. There are deserts with scrubby bushes and others with cactus forests. There are deserts covered with towering columns of strangely shaped rocks and others covered with salty lakes and salt flats.

A desert is formed by a particular combination of rainfall, temperature, location, and landscape. Each desert is distinct, yet all are alike in certain ways.

Deserts occupy one-seventh of the earth's surface and all of them have one thing in common: They are all dry. In fact, any place where the rainfall (or snowfall) is less than ten inches a year is called a desert. There are "polar deserts" in the Arctic and Antarctic, but this book is about deserts that are hot for at least part of the year.

Most deserts are found north and south of the equator in two narrow belts that circle the world. North of the equator, the great deserts are the Sahara, the Arabian, the Gobi, the Turkestan, the Indian, and the North American. South of the equator, the main deserts are the Kalahari, the Australian, the Patagonian, and the Atacama.

The four main North American deserts are the Great Basin, the Mojave, the Sonoran, and the Chihuahuan. While all are dry, the climate is different in each.

	GREAT BASIN
	MOJAVE DESERT
	SONORAN DESERT
	CHIHUAHUAN DESERT

THE NORTH AMERICAN DESERTS

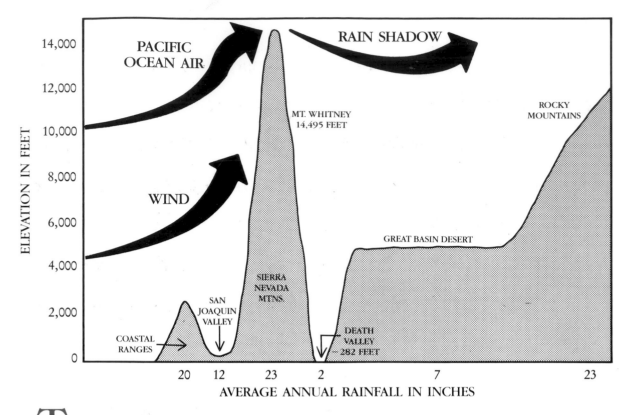

The North American deserts cover much of the southwestern United States and northern Mexico. These deserts are caused mainly by the "rain shadow" of mountains that lie across the path of the sea winds. Winds sweeping off the Pacific Ocean carry moisture inland. As the moist air is forced to rise over mountains, it cools down and can no longer hold as much water. Clouds form and rain falls on the upwind side of the mountains. The descending air on the downwind side of the mountains is drier and warmer. Very little rain falls here. Searing winds blow across the barren land, soaking up what little moisture there is and carrying it away.

White Sands National Monument in New Mexico is part of the Chihuahuan Desert, the largest desert in North America. Most of the Chihuahuan Desert lies in Mexico. Only a few hardy plants such as the yucca or creosote bush are able to grow in the parched soil of a sandy desert.

The largest and coolest desert in the United States is the Great Basin Desert. It lies in the "rain shadows" of the Sierra Nevada and Cascade mountain ranges, and covers much of Utah and Nevada, and parts of Oregon, Idaho, Wyoming, and other bordering states. The Great Basin is actually many smaller basins, each separated from the others by low mountain ranges. Small shrubs such as sagebrush and shadscale grow here.

Not all of the world's deserts are caused by the "rain shadow" effect. Moist warm air rises from regions around the equator and spreads north and south. High in the atmosphere, the air drops its moisture and becomes drier and heavier. The heavy air descends to the north around the Tropic of Cancer and to the south around the Tropic of Capricorn. In these areas, the prevailing winds are very dry because they have lost their moisture closer to the equator. It is here that most deserts are born.

The Sonoran Desert encircles the Gulf of California, from Baja California to western and southern Arizona and the Mexican state of Sonora. The western parts of the Sonoran Desert are very dry, while the eastern parts receive as much as ten inches of rain during the year. The climate determines what kinds of plants can grow there. Much of the Sonoran is home to the best-known of desert plants—the cactus.

Cacti are fleshy plants that store water in their stems. Like many cacti, this giant organ-pipe cactus in Arizona has a ribbed and grooved stem. When rain falls, the cactus's tissues fill with water and the plant expands like an accordion. The stored water allows the cactus to survive for many months without rain.

Even though deserts get little rain, rainstorms help shape the way they look. Monument Valley on the Arizona-Utah border was formed by sudden rainstorms and fierce winds over thousands of years. The flat-topped mountains, called mesas, rising hundreds of feet above the desert floor are remnants of the land in earlier times. The smaller tower-shaped rocks are called buttes, and the thin spires are called chimney or pipe rocks.

If rainfall in Monument Valley was spread evenly over the year, the rainwater would sink slowly into the soil, and grass could grow. But desert rains are short and violent, quickly soaking the top layer of soil. There is so much rain in such a brief time, the water doesn't have a chance to sink into lower layers, so it collects on the surface and begins to flow downhill. These flash floods rush down the hillsides, carrying along sand, rocks, and even boulders. The surging waters cut deep channels and gullies into the land.

The rushing waters may last for only an hour or two before they finally evaporate or sink into the desert floor miles away from the cloudburst. The flash floods leave behind gullies or arroyos—dry streambeds full of deposited sand and rocks. Then, once again, the desert is dry until the next cloudburst.

Rainwater flooding over the desert lands sometimes collects in low-lying spots, forming temporary lakes called playas. The water in a playa may be only a few inches deep but can cover hundreds of acres. A playa has no outlet, so most of the water evaporates into the air, while only a bit seeps into the hard ground. The evaporating water leaves behind a layer of salt on the surface of the ground. Only a few plants such as saltbush or pickerelweed can live in a playa such as this one in Death Valley. These plants have roots that grow deep beneath the salty crust of soil.

Natural rock bridges or arches in a desert are the result of erosion created by running water and windblown sand. Over thousands or even millions of years, an ancient river slowly wore down and undercut these red sandstone cliffs in Arches National Park in Utah. In time, the holes were enlarged and the arches were shaped by winds and rain.

Desert landscapes are forever being carved and reshaped, partly by the wind but mostly by the power of running water. The quickly moving waters of the Colorado River carry loose rocks and sand in a boiling torrent of white-water rapids. Year after year, century after century, the river grinds and scours its way through layers of rock, forming sheer-sided canyons or gorges.

For millions of years, the Colorado River has been at work, cutting out the Grand Canyon of Arizona. The riverbed is now more than a mile below the surrounding plateau.

Water shapes deserts in other ways, too. Over long periods of time, rainwater dissolves limestone rock and washes it away. Rainwater also dissolves calcium carbonate, the mineral that holds sandstone together. Then the grains of sand in sandstone are loosened and the rock becomes soft and easily worn down by the wind. The strange-looking sandstone towers of Utah's Bryce Canyon are the result of years of erosion caused by ancient rivers, rain and wind. In time, even these rock spires will be ground to dust.

During the day, air temperatures in a desert may soar above 100 degrees (F). Because there are few clouds to trap the stored heat near the ground, nighttime temperatures can plunge by thirty or forty degrees. Minerals in rocks expand when they are heated and contract when they cool down. The constant heating and cooling finally cracks the desert rocks into small pieces. Winds and rain continue to wear down the rocks into even smaller bits.

The rocks of a desert are finally broken down into grains of sand. The grains become smaller and rounder as the wind bounces and rubs them against one another.

As the grains are swept along, they form sand dunes. The wind moves the dunes and ripples the sands. The grains are swept up the windward side of the dunes, then tumble down the lee side, where the wind slows and swirls around.

As more sand is swept up the dune, the whole dune moves slowly in the direction of the wind. Over time, a sand dune changes in size, shape, and location. A dune can move fifty to one hundred feet or more in a year. Most of the sand dunes in American deserts are several hundred feet high, but dunes in the Sahara Desert may be one thousand feet high and stretch for miles.

Plants have different ways of surviving in a desert. A big saguaro cactus may store several tons of water after a heavy rain. The saguaro is the largest cactus in the American deserts. It grows slowly, but by the time a saguaro is over one hundred years old, it may be fifty feet tall and weigh more than ten tons.

Other desert plants, such as the Mexican goldpoppy, grow only after a heavy rainstorm. The seeds may remain for a year or longer in the desert soil. A light rain has no effect on them, but a heavy rain washes away the seeds' special coating and allows them to grow.

In a few short weeks, the seeds sprout, the plants grow quickly, and their flowers bloom. In the spring, blossoms may carpet the desert floor. Soon the plants wither and die, but not before they have produced seeds for future years' crops.

Just as plants have adapted in special ways to survive in the desert, so, too, have animals. The Gila woodpecker makes its home in a waterproof hole in the saguaro cactus. Feathers protect birds against the heat of the desert. Most birds feed during the cooler early-morning or early-evening hours and shelter in the shade during the hotter part of the day.

Some smaller desert animals such as rodents rarely drink. They get all the water they need from the seeds and stems they eat. Other animals such as snakes and lizards get their water from the animals upon which they prey. Many desert animals are nocturnal; they come out mainly during the night. Those that do move about in the scorching heat of the day keep their bodies high off the ground, sometimes by hopping or running on tiptoe.

Deserts are very different from the green farmlands, forests, and grassy spots that most people know. For some people, deserts are just dead lands of little interest. For other people, deserts are fascinating places. Deserts have some of the most beautiful landscapes in the world. And the canyons, rocks, and sand dunes are home for a great variety of plants and animals. For those who look closely, the desert is alive with mystery and wonder.

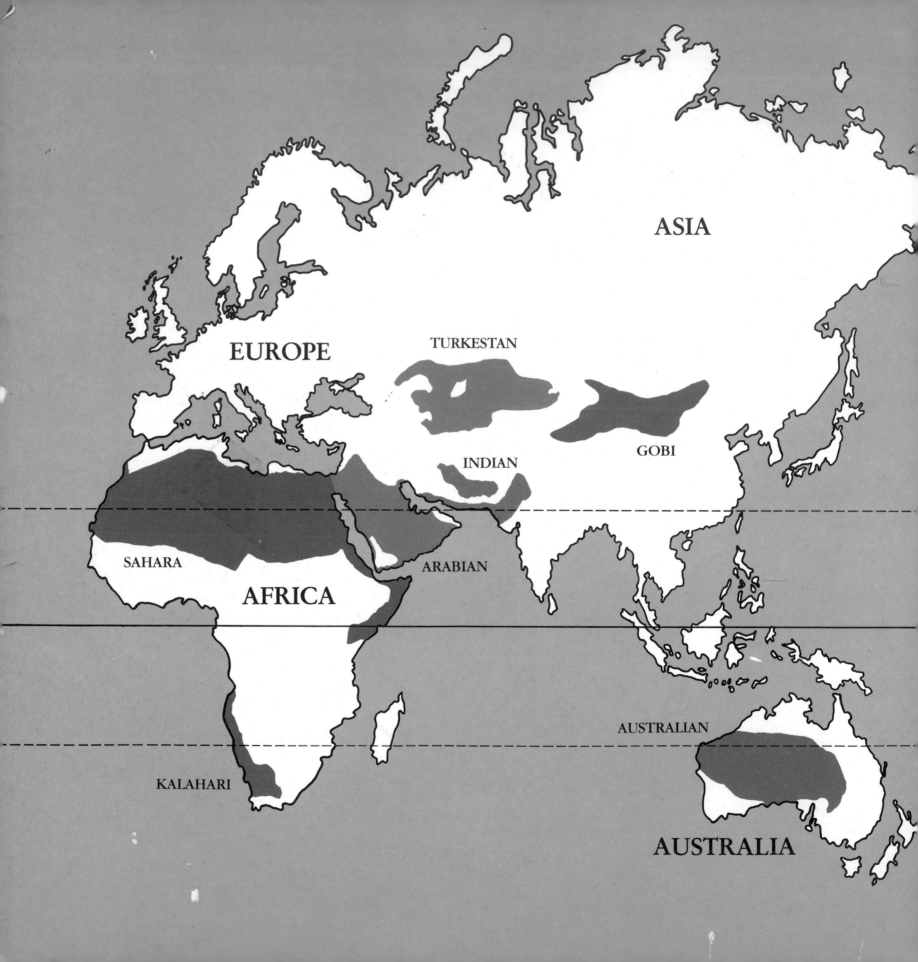

ASIA

EUROPE

TURKESTAN

GOBI

INDIAN

SAHARA

ARABIAN

AFRICA

KALAHARI

AUSTRALIAN

AUSTRALIA